CW01261489

Gloucester
in old picture postcards

by Reginald Woolford and Barbara Drake

European Library ZALTBOMMEL/THE NETHERLANDS

GB ISBN 90 288 3286 6 / CIP

© 1995 European Library – Zaltbommel/The Netherlands

No part of this book may be reproduced in any form, by print, photoprint, microfilm or any other means, without written permission from the publisher.

Introduction

The foundations of the centre of the City of Gloucester date to the late 60s AD when a Roman fort was constructed to provide the invading Roman army with access into Wales over a practicable crossing of the River Severn. This replaced an earlier fort built at Kingsholm to the north. Moving west to Caerleon, the army left a settlement of time-expired veteran soldiers, traders and camp followers, which in 96 AD was granted the status of a Colonia by Emperor Nerva to be called 'Colonia Nerva Glevensis', or Glevum for short. This high honour was shared by only three other places, Colchester, Lincoln and York. Sound administration and regular trade made for a successful community, and they left for us today, odd relics of their passing, not easy to find, but there if you search.

The Romans withdrew in 410 leaving the Britons to look to their own defences from eastern raiders, but the Anglo-Saxons (the fighters) soon overwhelmed the Britons (the farmers), became rulers and dictated terms. Gloucester became a town of the Mercian Kingdom of the Hwicce, and here King Osric founded a monastery in 679. Danish incursions followed, ending with Cnut, or Canute, being made King of Britain in 1016. In Gloucester, as a result of tactics to repel these forces when Queen Aethelflaeda refortified the town, a new layout of streets and lanes emerged, the ground plan of our present streets. She also founded the Minster Church of St. Oswald, where she laid the bones of the 7th century Northumbrian Saint. Remains of that church can be seen today.

In the time of Edward the Confessor, the town's status rose when the King and his Great Council met regularly at Westminster, Winchester and the Royal Palace at Kingsholm, as did William of Normandy when he claimed the throne and ruled the country. The Normans left us a legacy of sound government following the compilation of the Domesday Book, written here in Gloucester in 1085, and of secure strongholds – Gloucester Castle lies beneath H.M. Prison. His most notable legacy is to be seen in the Abbey Church of the Benedictine monastery of St. Peter that he founded – the huge pillars of the nave being just some of the rich features in this church that overlay Osric's church, designed by Abbot Serlo, and consecrated in 1100. The town continued to rank highly in Henry I's reign, so too when the boy king Henry III was crowned in the Abbey Church in 1216, favouring the town with gifts of wood from the Royal Forest of Dean for a Dominican and Franciscan Friary, remains of which can still be seen. When Edward II was so cruelly murdered in Berkeley Castle in 1327, the fortunes of the Abbey flourished when Abbot Thokey accepted the body to be buried, thus acquiring revenue for years to come from visitors on pilgrimage to the tomb – the exquisite fan tracery in the cloisters, the soaring tower.

With Henry VIIII's Dissolution of the monasteries, the Abbey Church became the Cathedral within the new Diocesan See of Gloucester. Other monasteries closed and the churches became private houses. His daughter, Mary, was determined to restore Roman Catholicism in a Protestant country and many clergy became martyrs for their faith, including Bishop Hooper, Bishop of Gloucester in 1555. His other daughter, Elizabeth, granted the town the status of a port in 1580, the most inland port in the country.

Gloucester stood out firmly against the Crown during the Civil War and suffered a 26-day siege in 1643 that greatly influenced the ending of hostilities, but as a result all its walls and gates were destroyed when Charles II was restored to the throne in 1660, because the people had raised arms against the King. The City's prowess in industry and social reform had far-reaching effect in the 18th and 19th centuries and as systems of transport improved, so did its importance. With the building of the Gloucester/Berkeley Canal and the creation of Gloucester Docks in the early 1800s, the vast warehouses for the storing of corn helped to feed the burgeoning Midlands. Timber was another commodity on which the good fortune of the City depended, creating employment for thousands of workers and thereby accelerating the growth of residential areas. Tourism is today's up-and-coming industry, creating more awareness of the wealth of this ancient City's past. Within these pages the camera has captured glimpses of a period of major expansion from 1880 to 1930, and the ordinary people who made it happen.

We are indebted to John Harris of Newent, G.K. Johnson of Gloucester and Alan Drewett of Churchdown, and to the following for the use of information from their books: Philip Moss *Historic Gloucester* 1993; John JuriËa *Gloucester. A Pictorial History* 1994; Jill Voyce *Gloucester in Old Photographs* 1985, 1989, Hugh Conway-Jones *Gloucester Docks* 1984; Pevsner *The Buildings of England. Gloucestershire: The Vale & Forest of Dean* 1970; The Victoria History of the County of Gloucester. Vol. IV 1988; Alan Moore *The Picture Palaces of Gloucester and Cheltenham* 1989; The Gloucestershire Record Office.

1   William the Conqueror founded a Benedictine order at Gloucester, the Abbey of St. Peter, designed by Abbot Serlo from Mont St. Michel, Normandy. The Abbey Church was consecrated in 1100 and overlaid the earlier 7th century church of the monastery of Osric, King of the Hwicce. On the restored south porch dating to the late 1800s, executed by J.F. Redfern, can be seen effigies of Osric in the lower right niche and Abbot Serlo on the left. The Abbey Church, later to become the Cathedral in 1541, gradually reached its splendid proportions over the centuries. The body of Edward II, cruelly murdered at Berkeley Castle, was brought to Gloucester for burial in 1327. Visitors made a pilgrimage to the tomb and their gifts and legacies had a significant effect on the fortunes of this great building.

2   The wooden choirstalls date from 1350. Intricately carved, they contain 58 misericord seats decorated with scenes that reflect the interest of their creators. The original Norman presbytery and choir were altered and enlarged early on in the 1300s, following major reconstruction work to the roof and body of the church. The vault of the new choir was raised to a height of 28.5 m (92 ft) thus making it the highest medieval stone vault in England. The roof bosses at the east end are decorated with fifteen angels, each one playing a different musical instrument. The great organ, completed in 1666, was resited in its present position in the 18th century. The wooden case was constructed by the Cathedral carpenters and it was gilded and painted by a local painter.

3   The fan tracery of the Great Cloister is the earliest known example in the country and dates from the 1350s. It is even more elaborate than that used by the masons for the richly-decorated choir of the church. The south walk contains twenty carrels or cubicles used by the Abbey monks for writing or study. The north walk, seen here, houses the monks' washing place or lavatorium that was supplied with fresh water, piped in from a spring on Robinswood Hill. The cloister is situated rather unusually on the north side of the Abbey Church. It was normal to use the warmer south aspect, but the close proximity of the town on the south meant it had to be built where space permitted.

4   Church House, north-west of the Cathedral, has a 13th century gabled front concealing the Norman Abbot's lodgings where the King and nobility were accommodated and entertained when visiting – Henry VIII and Ann Boleyn were the renowned visitors in July 1535. In the 14th century the Abbot had new premises built for himself on the north side of the precincts and this house was assigned to the Prior. The Abbot's Hall, as it is still known today, is divided into two large rooms, the Laud Room lined with fine Jacobean panelling, and the Henry Room with a painted and decorated ceiling.

5   The timber-framed building seen in this postcard is the Parliament Room. Richard II held Parliament at Gloucester in 1378. The tradition of holding Parliament here originated during the reign of Edward the Confessor. Winchester, Westminster and Gloucester were the three centres used, at Easter, Whitsun, and Christmas respectively. At the meeting in Gloucester in 1085 William the Conqueror ordered a detailed survey of the country that became known as the Domesday Book. Another house has been built to the left since the photograph was taken in Miller's Green. When the sun is in the west, this is an excellent place for a worthy picture.

6   These ruins are to be found to the north of the Cathedral. They are part of the 13th century south arcade and west wall of the Monastery Infirmary. Here not only the brethren were tended, but also the wealthy elderly people from the secular community – an old peoples' home, if you like. Following the Dissolution, this church-like building was subdivided and extended to provide accommodation in which to house the families of the canons and servants of the Cathedral – the area rudely being referred to as 'Babylon'.

7   In this postcard dated about 1910 the two buildings on the right, the Wilts & Dorset Bank on the southwest corner of the Cross and St. Michael's Church in Eastgate Street have undergone radical alteration. The Wilts & Dorset Bank was built on the site of the old Tolsey and opened in 1895. When the London City & Midland Bank was built on the northwest corner of the Cross, the two banks made a visual impact on the Cross, until Burtons, the outfitters, inserted large plate-glass windows and a heavy Welsh slate detail at ground floor level in the 1930s. St. Michael's fate was more ruthless, when the body of the church was demolished in 1956 leaving just the 15th century tower. The body of the church had been rebuilt in 1849, so had no antique value once St. Michael's had become redundant. The tower became the Tourist Information Centre in 1985.

THE CROSS, SHOWING ST MICHAELS CHURCH, GLOUCESTER.

8   Between 1905 and 1907 three shops were demolished on this northwest corner to make way for the London City & Midland Bank. Two further extensions were made into Westgate Street, the first necessitating the removal of Baker's boots and shoes, and Box & Co, jeweller, seen in this postcard. The second extension in the 1970s, by Keith Savery, won a Civic Award. Whilst excavating the foundations at that time the base of a Roman column was found, which now graces the foyer of the City Museum in Brunswick Road.

5   GLOUCESTER. — *Westgate Street* — LL.

9   This delightful view down Westgate Street was taken at the end of the last century. Victorian photographers needed long exposure time for their plate cameras, and the boy on the pavement, who is possibly taunting the lad in the road, forgets to stand still. They stand outside the Theatre Royal public house. Alterations have been made, but on the whole Westgate Street retains its character. A large redevelopment, however, can be seen on the right further down the street – this was when College Street was being widened, which dates this picture to 1893.

10   The Monk's Retreat lies beneath the Fleece Hotel in Westgate Street. The postcard states that 'it is part of a 12th century Benedictine Monastery'. The inn was one of their Pilgrim Hostels built for guests to the Abbey Church, but not until the 1450s. Legend has it that a tunnel existed between the Abbey and this cellar so that the monks could sneak out for a pint. But the tunnel proved to be nothing more than a bricked-up Victorian sewer – and anyway, the monks made all their own beer and probably supplied the inn too. It is, however, the only part of the early inn that remains.

The Monks' Retreat.
Part of a 12th Century Benedictine Monastery.
The Most Curious Bar in England.

Fleece Hotel,
Gloucester.

11   Entry into this lane off Westgate Street reveals one of Gloucester's finest remaining 16th century timber-framed buildings. Four storeys, with five gables on the side elevation, and leaded lights, many of which still retain their original glass and fittings. Known as Maverdine Lane since the 1450s, this was one of the 10th century streets created by Aethelflaeda of Mercia, daughter of Alfred the Great, at the time of the Danish invasions. In the early 19th century the house was called The Judges Lodgings, where Assize judges stayed when working at Gloucester. From 1886 to 1989 G. Winfield & Son, seed merchants, became a well-known name in the gardening world, trading at No. 26. It is now a bookshop.

12   From the right-hand side of this photograph: the Theatre Vaults public house and Pit Entrance; The Theatre Royal Opera House; Rees Jones, draper; Evans, hosier and haberdasher; and the large classical building on the corner of College Court (formerly a bank), Beavens & Sons Ltd., plumbers, glaziers and sanitary engineers (now by Westgate Bridge as lighting and electrical engineers). The County of Gloucester Bank was built in the late 1830s at a time of economic development in the City and surrounds. The Gloucestershire Banking Company in Eastgate Street was of the same date.

The building was demolished in the late 1930s for British Home Stores.

13   This theatre, situated in Westgate Street, above College Court, opened on 6th June 1791. It became known as The Theatre Royal from the late 1830s and was enlarged over the years under various owners. In 1903 it was acquired by Pooles (of Myriorama fame) and the name changed to The Palace. It remained as a theatre until 1922, when Woolworths took over the property, remaining until 1970. They then moved into premises previously occupied by Blinkhorns. During the Theatre's lifetime many famous artists 'trod the boards'. It celebrated its centenary in 1891 with a performance by Henry Irving, Ellen Terry and members of the Lycium company in aid of the local hospitals. The site is now occupied by the store Poundstretcher.

14   Welch & Wicks, 20 Westgate Street, stood on the corner of Bull Lane. They were stationers selling postcards, newspapers and magazines. A closer scrutiny of the shelves in the window reveals other items – picture frames, evening bags, clothes brushes, ornaments and other knick-knacks that one finds in any stationers today. Fred Winfield, next door, was a florist who began trading here in 1906, a relative of the Winfields at No. 26. Urns full of flowers, flowering pot plants, plants on the ledge outside, made this a particularly colourful shop.

15 The steps to the left lead up to the Shirehall, which went through two phases of major expansion; one 1909-1911 with the subsequent demolition of the buildings to the left of the steps and into Berkeley Street; the second in the 1960s to the right. The jettied building on the right of the street is W.F. Saunders, outfitters, established 1868. Healey & Son was a carriage works, though by this time a motor garage – not many of those about! Some ladies can be seen to the left of the street entering their carriage, having visited Mr. Wilton, the watchmaker.

16   Recording the building works during the first phase of expansion of the Shirehall in 1909. Robert Smirke designed this very classical building in 1816, with Ionic columns that are a small-scale replica of the British Museum in London, that he also designed. It replaced an earlier Shirehall. Even in those days the paperwork involved in the running of the day-to-day administration of County matters necessitated enlarging the building, not once, but twice within 180 years.

17   King Edward VII passes down Westgate Street on his way to the Royal Agricultural Show being held on the Oxlease below Westgate Bridge. The cavalry are opposite the Shirehall, at the time when the building was being extended towards Berkeley Street, so it was not looking its best for the occasion. The bunting and the flags decorate the streets on this momentous and historic day, 23rd June 1909, whilst the ladies in their wonderful hats add a touch of elegance to the scene.

18   The buildings on the left were demolished for the second extension of the Shirehall in the 1960s. Here we see from the left: W. Wilton, watchmaker; The Booth Hall Hotel, the Old Bear inn, R. Meadows (fishmonger), the Brewer's Arms, and F.A. Meadows (hairdresser). Behind the hotel once stood a large medieval market hall called the Boothall in 1216, the principal leather and wool market, a hundred court and a piepowder court for settling petty grievances on the spot. It was rebuilt in 1529 for a Shirehall, the timber-framed front being refaced in 1742, with the city coat-of-arms in the pediment. After the new Shirehall opened, it was variously used as a music hall, skating rink, theatre, and finally a cinema – as seen here.

GLOUCESTER. ST. NICHOLAS CHURCH, WESTGATE STREET.

19 The 13th century Church of St. Nicholas came into the care of the Churches Conservation Trust in 1975, following the unification of the parish with that of St. Mary de Lode. Within the church are round Norman pillars at the west end of the nave, and 17th and 18th century funerary monuments and floor slabs recording the trades and professions within the parish. A few of these are of Mayors and aldermen dating to the time when the corporation had a serious dispute with the Dean and Chapter from 1738 to 1751, using St. Nicholas' Church instead of the Cathedral. Due to damage to the spire at the time of the Civil War and subsequent deterioration, John Bryan redesigned the part above the coronet in 1783. The whole church leans noticeably to the north.

20   This building, now part of the Folk Museum, was traditionally identified as Bishop Hooper's last lodging place before his martyrdom in 1555. Born in 1495 and living at a time of religious upheaval, he was greatly influenced by the extreme Protestants of his time. Made Bishop of Gloucester in 1551, he imposed a severe disciplinary regime. He became caught up in Queen Mary's determined efforts to stamp out Protestantism. He failed to recant and was condemned to death. His armed guards brought him 'to the house of Robert Ingram opposite the steeple of the Church', to spare him further humiliation at Northgate gaol. On 9th February 1555 he was taken to St. Mary's Square to be burnt at the stake. The rest I leave to Foxe's Book of Martyrs.

21   All the buildings seen in this postcard dated 1902 were demolished in 1907 in order to widen the road. The cause of the bottle-neck was the old bridge called Foreign Bridge that lay just east of today's Westgate Car Park. This delightful timber-framed building, then Thomas Green, trunkmaker, was swept away unnoticed – in the name of improvement.

22 This is the west end of the row of buildings that were demolished in 1907. Standing several yards proud of the Iron & Hardware Co. premises (seen right) is W.T. Clutterbuck & Co, maltsters, built upon the footings of Foreign Bridge. Little Severn, later known as Dockham Ditch, was crossed here by a substantial bridge which had seven stone arches about 1540. As the volume of water decreased so parts of the bridge were built on. In 1825 the ditch was culverted below the bridge and the northern part filled as part of a programme of sanitary improvements in the city. The street frontage was set back to lie flush with the Iron Foundry premises.

23   Known as the Round House, this structure, built in 1694, was once the base of a large conical Glasshouse in Lower Westgate Street. Glass-making was one of several industries to be found in that area. Glass bottles for the local Gloucestershire and Herefordshire cider manufacturers, pickle jars, butter pots and melon glasses were produced. The venture came to an end in 1744 following the death of the manager of the business, John Platt. Competition from Bristol was also blamed for its failure to become firmly established. The Round House was converted into tenements, but in later years it was used as a warehouse. It was demolished in 1933.

24   In this view of Lower Westgate Street, dated 1904, only two buildings remain. On the right is the Royal Oak inn with the tenements of Royal Oak yard behind, and a lodging house – all gone, to be replaced by Beaven & Son, electrical engineers. Part of the modern gyratory road system is known as Royal Oak Road. The buildings, formerly Dan Smith, baker and mealman, and his warehouse, remain. The Pineapple inn was demolished in 1972. The timber-framed building, dismantled in the 1960s, was sent out of the country. J. Cratchley, haulier and coal merchant, with Goodrich Court lying behind through the arch, W. Cole, hairdresser, and a general shop next door, have gone. Today West Midland Farmers occupy the area.

25 When a new bridge to cross the Severn was being constructed in Gloucester in the 12th century, the workmen were accommodated in a hostel, which later became a hospice for the sick, and gave shelter to travellers, run by a priest, known as the Hospice of St. Bartholomew the Apostle. By 1789 the building was old and ruinous so the corporation rebuilt it as an Almshouse, set further back from the roadway. Designed by William Price in a Gothic style, the chimneys and bell tower gave it character, that today it sadly lacks. It had its own chapel, consecrated by the Bishop of Gloucester in 1790 – where today wines and spirits are sold. The building was sold by the Charity Trustees in 1971, and opened as the Westgate Galleria, a shopping and craft centre, on 23rd August 1985.

26   An aerial view of Gloucester from the south-west showing the Cathedral and River Severn. Dated 1920 the photograph was taken from an *AIRCO 9b machine* flying over the town and published by the Aircraft Manufacturing Co. Ltd., Hendon. Barges wait alongside the slipways at the Quay and a steam traction-engine tows three wagons. The coal wharf is clearly visible to the left, along with the Old Customs House, the square stone building. The white building on the quay is The Mermaid, the sailor's pub from 1806 to 1929. How different it all looks today!

27　This 1908 advertisement for the *Windsor Castle* states that 'it is licensed to carry 217 passengers'. It gives us an unique view into town from the Bridge, and shows the Sabrina Cottages built by the river in the 1850s, and two public houses, The Bridge inn to the left of the road and the Forester's Arms to the right. The chimney would be on the site of Healey & Son Ltd., carriage works, formerly Arnold Gee & Co., matchworks. This area was radically altered in the 1970s when the new Westgate Bridge was built.

28 The steam packet *Lapwing* and its sister boat *Wave* gave pleasure trips on the Severn above Gloucester to Tewkesbury and Worcester, or along the canal. The return fare in 1909 to Sharpness was 9d (4p) first class, and 7d (3p) second class. Two other boats, the steam launch *Berkeley Castle*, built at Gloucester by Charles Priday in 1879, and its sister, the *Windsor Castle*, launched 1887, were also used. Here we see one of the Castle boats sailing up river having just passed under Westgate Bridge. Skiffs could be hired for a row from Hipwood's boat yard.

29 An exhibition of flying skills and potential was given by B.C. Hucks when he visited the Port Ham on 16th October 1911. One of the earliest aviators, he flew his *Blackburn Monoplane* to a height of 1,000 ft and is seen here back on *terra firma* being welcomed by the Mayor, James Bruton, and the City Corporation. Just nearby, on the city side of Westgate Bridge, was the Westgate Ironworks, where Webb, Peet & Co., aeronautical engineers, were the holders of valuable patents for valve gear of rotary aeroplane engines. At the time of auction, due to bankruptcy in 1913, a Gloucester Military Aeroplane and an incomplete Tandem monoplane, amongst other items, were part of the lots.

MR. B. C. HUCKS, AVIATOR AT GLOUCESTER, OCTOBER 1911.

30   This picture was taken a few years after College Street was widened in 1893 by the Gloucester Cathedral Approaches Company. It had been a very narrow street, with the 13th century lichgate into the Abbey precincts, known as King Edward's Gate, part of which survives. The main entrance into the Abbey was through St. Mary's Gate to the west. However, it became necessary to improve vehicular access to the Cathedral, and the company replaced all the buildings on the east side of the street by a uniform range of red brick shops with timber gables designed by Waller & Son, set some 4 to 5 m (15 ft) back from the original road frontage.

31   St. Michael's Gate in College Court led into the Lay Cemetery within the Abbey precincts and was built at the same period as the lich-gate in College Street. It became known as St. Michael's Gate in 1649. The lane has been variously called Craft's Lane, Ironmonger's Row, Turries Lane and St. Peter's Lane. It became Upper College Lane in the 18th century. The first time it was called College Court was in 1778. The gate was one of only three entrances through the precinct walls in the middle ages. Today, the little shop to the left of the gate is the Beatrix Potter Museum. In her book *The Tailor of Gloucester* this gate features in one of the drawings as the fictional tailor's house. John Pritchard, the tailor on whom the book is based, worked at No. 23 Westgate Street.

32   This is College Court seen from St. Michael's Gate looking back towards Westgate Street, when the building, originally the County of Gloucester Bank, was still standing on the left corner, where Beaven & Son had their business. When it was demolished and British Home Stores erected on the site in the late 1930s, the whole of the left side of the lane was merely a high, blank red brick wall, that remained until the area was redeveloped in the 1980s and shops were re-instated. Sydney Pitcher was a well-known photographer, and many of his picture postcards are in circulation, such as these two of College Court.

33   This view towards the Cathedral overlooks Berkeley Street and the many buildings that lie between Longsmith Street, in the foreground, and Westgate Street. It was taken from the top of the Electricity Works chimney about 1909. To the left are the polygonal Courtrooms to the rear of the Shirehall designed in 1816 by Robert Smirke. The left side of Berkeley Street was demolished soon after this photograph was taken, for the extension of the Shirehall. The north side and much of the right side of Berkeley Street have been replaced by the Telephone Exchange.

34   Berkeley Street – and that innovation we now take for granted, the telephone. It took nearly a decade to get its potential across to the people of Gloucester. The Telegraph Company was established in 1878 with the Post Office enjoying a monopoly in the communications field. By June 1880 two local firms were using the telephone system at their businesses: the Gloucester Wagon Company and Messrs. Foster Bros, the oil mills. In 1881 the government gave the Post Office the go-ahead to offer telephones to the general public and a somewhat haphazard network began to develop. By 1887 the Gloucester Local Telephone Exchange was set up by the Western Counties & South Wales Telephone Co. Ltd. at 9 Berkeley Street with the first 16 subscribers connected. The trunk line between Gloucester and Bristol was officially opened on 6 July 1887.

35   A relic of past years. This building stood in Berkeley Street, on the east side between Westgate Street and Longsmith Street. No. 13, next door, was the premises of Arnold Perret Co., a local wines and spirits company. The site is now part of the Telephone Exchange complex.

36   Bull Lane, one of the 10th century lanes off Westgate Street, takes its name from The Bull inn, the projecting building by the gent on the pavement, built about 1700. In the 13th century the lane was called Gore Lane, due to the proximity of the slaughter houses – thankfully, they altered the name! Access to the rear of The Fleece inn was gained through the double doors to the right. Stabling, and today garaging, lay within.

Bull Lane, Gloucester   23930

37   Bearland House is a fine early 18th century brick-built house with an ornamental façade, forecourt and decorative wrought-iron railings and gates. It once had extensive formal gardens and orchards, but these gradually disappeared under subsequent development, and the house has been put to a variety of uses. It became the depot for the local militia in 1856, and a School of Art, instigated by Thomas Gambier Parry, in 1859. The estate was sold to the City corporation in 1899 and the City Electricity Works was constructed right behind the house in 1900. The Girls' Lower or Endowed School moved to Bearland House in 1904 from Barton Street and then on to Denmark Road, renamed the Girls' High School, in 1909. Today it is an office.

38   It took the Victorians to record the execution of Bishop Hooper in the form of this extravagant monument, 300 years after the event. Born in 1495 and entering upon his lifetime career in the ministry at a time of intense religious turmoil, this Protestant clergyman, who became Bishop of Gloucester in 1551, fell foul of Queen Mary's Catholic fervour. By refusing to recant, he was sentenced to be burnt at the stake in Gloucester. This monument is reputed to stand on the exact spot of his execution, and replaces an earlier memorial placed there in 1826 in the form of a small tomb by J.R. Cleland of Co. Down. This more substantial monument, paid for by public subscription in 1861-1863, was designed by J. Medland & A.W. Maberly, with an effigy of the bishop by Edward Thornhill.

39 The view in this Christmas card dated 1904 was taken from the tower of St. Mary de Lode Church and looks over St. Mary's Square and Bishop Hooper's monument. The buildings to the right were demolished in the 1950s. The 13th century main entrance into the Abbey precincts, St. Mary's Gate, nestles beside the lodging house of the Abbey Almoner to the right, a 16th century timber-framed building on the walls of a 13th century undercroft. Left-overs from the monks' meal were dispensed as alms to the poor of the city from an opening that lies behind the window next to the gateway.

Gloucester Cathedral
May we soon meet again. Meanwhile;
The heartiest of Christmas Greetings.

Valentines Series

From Mr. & Mrs. Gastrell Phillips,
Sunnyside, Gloucester.

40   St. Mary's Gate, or the 13th century Great Gate, was the main entrance into the Abbey precincts until a new entrance to the Cathedral was created in College Street in the late 1890s. The gable is decorated with arcading and has transitional Norman vaulting within the archway. From these windows overlooking St. Mary's Square, the Dean and Chapter and other officials witnessed the martyrdom of Bishop Hooper in 1555. Today, the timbers of the adjoining 16th century Almoner's lodging house have been exposed, thus making the building more attractive and well photographed.

41 The dedication of St. Mary de Lode refers to a river crossing, over Old Severn, a channel of the Severn long since gone. In the Middle Ages it was referred to as 'St. Mary before the Abbey Gate' and in the 16th century 'St. Mary Broadgate', the main entrance into the Abbey of St. Peter, which lay east of the church. The chancel and tower survive from the medieval church of pre-Conquest origin and the body of the church from a rebuilding in the 1820s. When the foundations of the nave were being re-laid, a Roman building was revealed. According to local tradition it was the burial place of Lucius, who died four years after his conversion to christianity in the reign of the Roman Emperor, Marcus Aurelius, in 105 AD. In 1643 the church was used as a prison for Royalist soldiers and in the 18th century the spire on the tower blew down in a violent storm.

42   The interior of St. Mary de Lode Church reflects its antiquity. The rather tunnel-like chancel contains two arches, the first being Norman, the second 13th century, with a vaulted ceiling. The difference in scale between the old building and subsequent rebuilding is very marked. A broad nave supported by cast-iron columns was built on to the Norman building in 1826 by James Cooke, of Gloucester, who was also a monumental mason. The 18th century organ was brought from St. Nicholas' Church, Westgate Street, in 1972.

43   Most churches in the 1920s and 1930s boasted large choirs – boys, men and ladies. This picture taken in 1928 shows the choir of St. Mary de Lode with the Vicar, Reverend W.G. Pritchard, in the centre. The two churchwardens holding their staves of offices are Mr. Jackson, left, and Mr. White, then Governor of H.M. Prison, Gloucester. St. Mary de Lode Church has the oldest foundation of all the city churches.

44   These ivy-covered walls are all that remain of a 10th century Minster Church founded by Aethelflaeda, daughter of Alfred the Great, and her husband, Aethelred, Lord of the Mercians, as a shrine for the relics of St. Oswald of Northumbria, killed at the Battle of Maserfield in 641. It became an Augustinian Priory in the 12th century, the north transcept and aisle of its church being converted into the Parish Church of St. Catherine after the Dissolution. Parts of the priory buildings were incorporated into a dwelling house called The Priory for the Reverend John Newton about 1770, but were demolished in 1823-1824. St. Catherine's was rebuilt adjacent to the ruins in 1867, but demolished in 1921 when the parish was transposed to Wotton, north of the city, in 1915, leaving just this one wall standing, dating to 909 AD.

45 It is a pleasure to look at the following postcards of Eastgate Street taken at a time when the street had its own unique character and charm. Today only the group of three Victorian buildings, the Guildhall, Lloyds, and National Westminster Banks, along with the Market Portico, enrich the rather bland modern street scene. Lloyds Bank, built in 1898 by Waller & Son, of red brick and terracotta, can be seen beside the tram on the left, the Market Portico, 1856, opposite. The Greyhound Hotel, later Botherways, and then the Cadena, stood beside St. Michael's Church, of which only the tower remains.

46   In this picture, taken before the days of electricity, the Market Portico is the prominent feature. Built in 1856 to a design by James Medland and A.W. Maberly, it comprised one large hall for the daily produce market, with this massive, pedimented entrance supported by large Corinthian columns. Gradually the regular stallholders ousted the country people with baskets of produce. Eastgate Market Hall was taken down in the late 1960s for the development of a modern shopping centre with its own integral market area, which opened in 1968. This portico was re-sited as the main entrance 40 m west of its original site.

47   The Guildhall, opened in 1892 on the site formerly occupied by Sir Thomas Rich's School (or Blue Coat School, founded 1666). Designed by George Hunt, the stone façade is decorated at attic level with heraldry and cherubs. The Council's quarters at the Tolsey in Westgate Street had become too cramped, which necessitated the move to larger and more convenient premises. It remained in Civic use until 1985, when the Council moved once more to a converted warehouse at Gloucester Docks. Next to the Guildhall stood the newly-rebuilt Saracen's Head Hotel (now demolished), forming an impressive group of Victorian architecture.

48   When the National Provincial Bank was built in Eastgate Street in 1888, this delightful old town house was demolished. It had been occupied by the furniture business of Richard Margrett & Son. Formerly it had been the town house of the Crawley-Boeveys of Flaxley, and at some other time occupied by Mrs. Delany, a friend of Queen Charlotte, wife of George III. The bank building, which today is the National Westminster, has a stone front in classical style designed by Charles Gribble of London.

49   Date stamped 1913, this postcard shows on the left the successful drapery business of Robert Blinkhorn, opened in Eastgate Street in 1843, attracting many shoppers. Next door was The Three Cups Dining Rooms. The brewery dray is delivering to The Market House pub. The Central Hotel, on the corner of King Street, was another City centre hotel.

50   This was an everyday scene in Eastgate Street in about 1908 – tram, delivery van and shoppers. The taller of the buildings on the right was the American & Canadian Stores, selling leather goods and furs. Next door to the left is The Rising Sun public house that became the City Cinema in 1911, closing in 1961. Blinkhorns is the shop on the left with all the lamps.

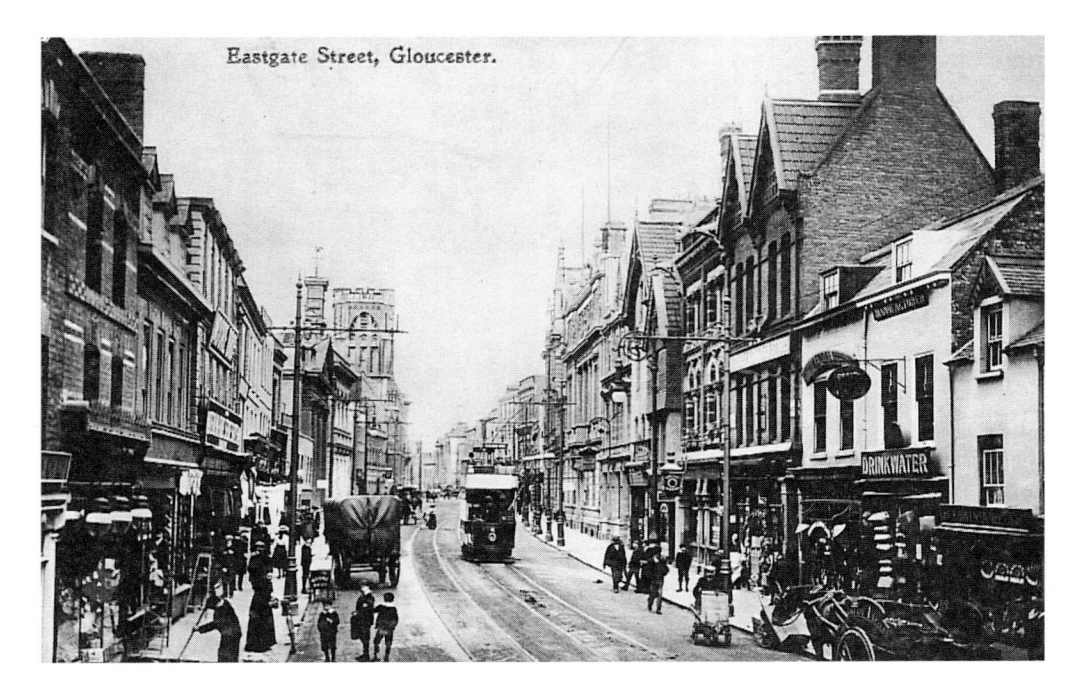

51   The City Cinema, one of the early Picture Palaces, occupied a site in Eastgate Street – now the British Home Stores. It was originally constructed on the site of the Rising Sun public house, owned by three very well-known Gloucester business men: Messrs. Bayliss, Rasbach and Kiddle. The opening date was 20th June 1911. Following improvements carried out in 1914, it re-opened on 1st March 1915 renamed The Hippodrome. In 1922 it was acquired by Pooles, a well-known entertainment firm who retained the premises until Ranks took over the property in 1956, as The Gaumont. A disastrous fire took place on 23rd October 1955, but the building re-opened in June 1956. The cinema finally closed on 22nd April 1961.

52   Eastgate Street about 1925 looking towards the Cross from Brunswick Road. The building on the right is Eastgate House, built by John Ricketts junior about 1781, soon after the medieval Eastgate was taken down. John came from the family of monumental sculptors who executed some fine memorials in the Cathedral and parish churches elsewhere. John Bellows built his printing works to the rear of the house in 1873, where he produced maps as well as books. The building was demolished about 1970 during the King's Walk Shopping Arcade development. To the left of Eastgate House, on the corner of King Street, can be seen the City Hotel.

53   This building was situated on the corner of Brunswick Road and Eastgate Street, a site now occupied by Boots the chemists. The firm was established in 1860 and had a number of branches throughout South Wales. In 1885 they had premises at 146 Westgate Street, between College Court and the old Theatre Royal, and had moved to Eastgate Street about 1900. The business was taken over before 1920 by Wallace Harris, who also had a shop in Westgate Street No. 11. In latter years, before the site was redeveloped, it was in use as a shop for the Midlands Electricity Board.

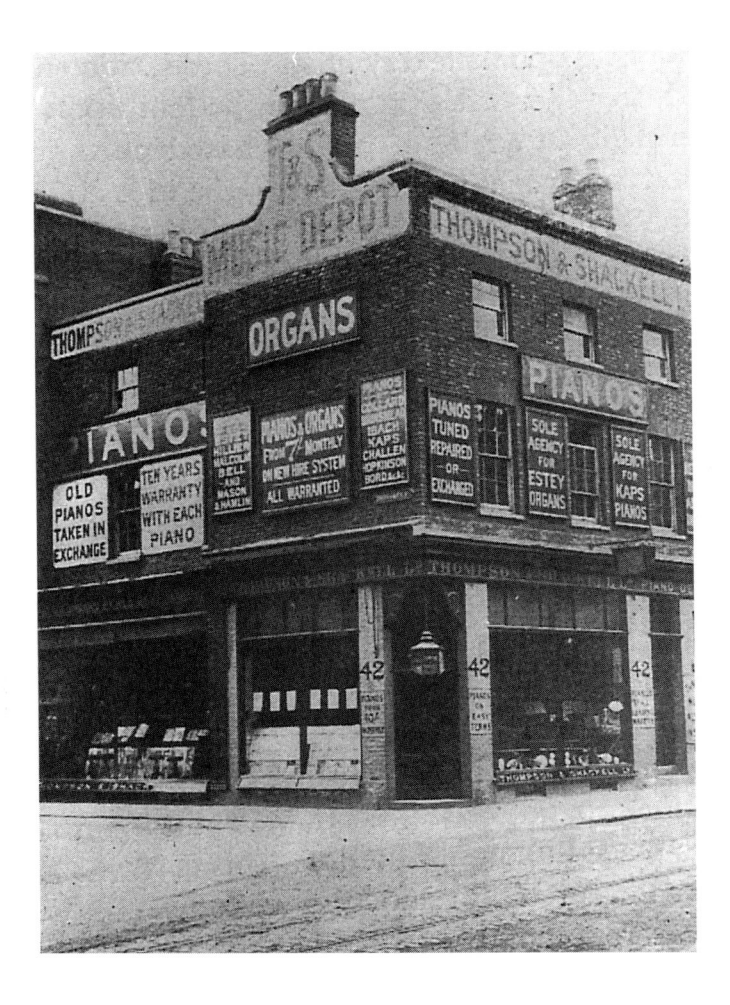

54   This group is Wallace Harris' Banjo and Mandoline Band in 1907. Used as a postcard, it was sent by 'Emmie', who refers to it as 'our group' to her friend, Lily James. Which of the ladies is Emmie? Four banjo players and eight mandolines plus a gent at the piano – could that be Wallace Harris himself? He certainly was into pianos as a business by the 1920s. Bands like this one were becoming very popular at the time, giving musical entertainment in halls, tea-houses, etc.

55   Joseph Beard began trading at 43, Eastgate Street in about 1889, remaining there until W.H. Smith took over the premises in 1952. They in turn moved further up the street to avail themselves of a prime site within the King's Walk Arcade in the 1970s. Beards prided themselves on being the 'Central House for Postcards, Maps and Guides' as well as being the depot for the British and Foreign Bible Society, newsagent, stationer and bookseller. Mudies Circulating Library would have been similar to the Boot's Lending Library, and available in any small bookshop.

56   When King Edward VII visited Gloucester in June 1909 for the Royal Agricultural Show, such was the eager anticipation of the locals to catch a glimpse of their monarch – probably the only time they would ever see him – that they used any vantage point possible – take a close look at the roof-tops. The photograph was taken in Eastgate Street as the King was either just arriving at the Guildhall to meet the civic leaders, or just departing on his way to the Showground on the Oxlease.

57   This picture is of one of the City's former elegant town houses in Barton Street, now Eastgate Street, Elton Hall. Built in the 18th century, with elaborate gardens, it was the residence of Dr. James Forbes, the first Unitarian Minister in Gloucester; later Charles Greville, physician, and in the 20th century Ernest Dykes Bower, surgeon and oculist. It was demolished in 1921 to make way for an extension to the Co-op building seen to the right. That was demolished and replaced by a modern store which opened in 1931. Other buildings to the left were demolished to allow the construction of The Plaza Cinema, which opened in November 1935, later to become the Odeon and now the Top Rank Bingo Club.

58 Barton Street (now Eastgate) looking east, seen in the early days of the electric trams. The groups of people on either pavement wait for their trams, it just being possible to make out the tram stop signs. Such is the leisurely speed of transport that the lady on her bicycle is quite safe passing the traffic on the wrong side! The man with the hand-cart would probably be delivering bread. On the right of the picture is Elton House, now demolished and the site of the Co-op. On the left, Norville's, opticians, is just visible, which continues in the same premises today.

59   Designed by Mr. J. Fletcher Trew, a Gloucester architect, the Public Baths in Barton Street (now Eastgate) were opened in July 1891 at a cost of over £10,000. The building was of a plain, substantial character, built chiefly of Cattybrook bricks with self-finished facings both inside and out. There were two swimming baths, both 100' x 50', one of which was convertible as a gymnasium or skating rink, and fourteen private baths. The Turkish baths were, according to an advertisement, 'recognised to be the best of their kind in the West of England'.

60   A view looking up Brunswick Road taken from the entrance to St. Michael's Square. Many important late 19th century public buildings can be found here – the School of Science and Art, 1871; the site of Raikes' Memorial Hall, 1884; the Price Memorial Hall, 1892, a tribute to William Price by his wife Margaret; the Public Library, 1898, which is an extension of the Science and Art School. St. Michael's Square was laid out in 1882 by Daniel Pidgeon of Putney. St. Michael's Vicarage stood on one corner of the square, and the turreted house seen in the photograph was at one time the residence of Reverend Belmont Naylor.

61 This quiet, leafy road south of the City led to the Spa Pump Room. Called Parker's Row, later Brunswick Road, much of this area was developed residentially with villas and terraced housing, following the discovery of a spring of saline water and its subsequent creation into a Spa in May 1815. The vapour baths fell into disrepair and were removed in 1894 and the Pump Room ceased to dispense water in 1926 following contamination. The building was demolished in 1960. Just one pineapple finial is left as a memorial to a short period in an age of elegance.

62   Spa Road was THE fashionable place to live when the street, formerly Norfolk Street, was being laid out with large villas in 1816. A tree-lined street, open ground to the south laid out as a park, yet only a few minutes from the City centre. In this postcard the Pump Room of 1815, where medicinal waters were dispensed, can be seen to the right. Hot and cold vapour baths, which were the vogue when the Spa was in its hey-day, were available too. Though the Spa has long since gone, the street retains its dignity.

THE SPA, GLOUCESTER.

63   This building, which was to become a well-known establishment to many former 'young ladies' of Gloucester, was one of the first buildings to be erected when the owners of the Spa were developing the area. The Spa Hotel, at the west end of Spa Road, was built in 1818 as a boarding house for visitors to the Spa. It was later known as Ribston Hall. In 1921 the United Schools governors opened Ribston Hall High School as a second Girls' High School. It became a Secondary Grammar School under the 1944 Act and moved to new buildings in Stroud Road in 1961. Until recently GlosCAT have used the building as an annex.

64   A busy scene at the Cross, Southgate Street in about 1910: a tram, three horse-drawn conveyances and many pedestrians. To the left of the Bell Hotel is a delightful Jacobean timber façade, originally the town house of Thomas Yate, apothecary, still much admired. In the late 18th century laundry 'blue' was sold here – the shop was painted blue! On the roof is an enormous metal tea-caddy – Mr. Clark, tea merchant, sold a choice stock of Indian and Ceylon teas. The arched opening further left contains the mechanical clock of G.A. Baker, clockmaker, an attraction since 1904. The mechanism was manufactured by Neihus Bros. of Bristol, with striking figures representing England, Wales, Scotland and Ireland, with Old Father Time in the centre.

65   The electric trams still ply their routes, but horses have given way to motors, in this view of Southgate Street in about 1930. The chauffeur waits patiently in the open tourer, whilst a more opulent number stands outside the Bell Hotel. A young mother holds her little boy for the benefit of the photographer. On the roof-line on the left can be seen a figure. This was the statue of Ceres that surmounted the Corn Exchange. Designed by Medland & Maberly in 1856 with a semi-circular portico of tall Corinthian columns, it was re-fronted flush with the street frontage in 1893.

66   Electricity was to have a profound effect all over the globe. Everyone would notice this technological innovation in so many aspects of their daily life – things that today we take for granted. Lighting and transport would be noticed by even the poorest person, even if there was no personal use of it. When the Electricity Generating Station was opened in Commercial Road in 1900, the very first street light to be installed was this one on the corner of Westgate and Southgate Streets, where these men watch the installation of the Electric Tramway in 1904.

67 The Bell Hotel in Southgate Street was one of the leading City centre hotels until its closure in 1967 for the development of the Bell Walk Shopping Arcade. Mentioned in 1544, the long pedimented front was added about 1793. Its greater claim to fame was that the 18th century evangelist George Whitfield was born here in 1714 – his father was the innkeeper. A pot-boy as a child, George went on to preach about 18,000 sermons to an estimated ten million people in his lifetime both in England and America. The Bell was the official stopping point for the London Mail Coach by the late 18th century.

68   This decorative 16th century timber-framed house in Southgate Street was from 1768 to 1801 the home of Robert Raikes, founder of the Sunday School Movement. It has unusual barge-boards in the gables, inspired by yolks. Oxen wore yolks to pull the traces of the plough which tilled the soil, the grain was harvested and the bread was baked for the baker's shop. The dairy-maid carried her pails of milk either end of the yolk around her neck, which became butter, cream or cheese for the grocer's shop. At first floor level three conical sugar-loaves, a traditional sign for a grocer's shop – whichever way you look at it, it's a provisions store!

69   This view to the Cross in Southgate Street in 1921 shows the Ram Hotel, now The New County, originally one of three pilgrim hostels built by the Abbey to accommodate the increasing number of visitors to the Abbey Church of St. Peter. Nothing of the original fabric remains. This building was refronted in 1890. In the 1790s it ranked high among the City inns and in 1822 was one of the five principal establishments running coaches to staging points.

70   One of Symond's horse-drawn omnibuses stands awaiting passengers in this view up Southgate Street, dated 1905, taken from the junction with Commercial Road. The Church of St. Mary de Crypt, complete with battlements and pinnacles, adds a certain character, which the street now lacks since their removal. The Berkeley Hunt public house can be seen on the right.

71 It is the battlemented tower of St. Mary de Crypt Church in Southgate Street that catches the eye in this postcard, with its immense pinnacles – the more so because only a very few people remember them. They were removed in 1908 as being unsafe along with the battlements and never replaced, so the tower always looks incomplete and disfigured. The church is notable, however, in its connection with George Whitfield, the well-known 18th century evangelist. He preached his first sermon, the start of a long career in which he travelled thousands of miles, not only in this country but also in America. Much of the fabric of the church dates to an extensive restoration carried out by S.W. Daukes and J.R. Hamilton in the 1840s.

72   Built in 1755 to a design by Luke Singleton, the Gloucester Infirmary in Southgate Street was financed by subscriptions, gifts and legacies. George II donated timber from the Forest of Dean and the infirmary was visited in 1788 by George III. It took over the work of the Gloucestershire Eye Institution in 1878 and was granted the title the Gloucestershire Royal Infirmary & Eye Institution by Edward VII in 1909. It amalgamated with the Gloucester City General Hospital when the National Health Service was introduced in 1948 and it became known as the Gloucester Royal Hospital. A new general hospital was built in Great Western Road, with an eleven-storey tower-block, in the early 1960s. The wards at the Southgate building closed in 1975 and the building was demolished in 1984 to make way for the Bank of England premises.

73 A view up Lower Southgate Street about 1907. The Gloucester Royal Infirmary lay behind the trees, with Southgate Congregational Chapel opposite. Built in 1850 to a 14th century design by James Medland, it replaced an earlier chapel built in 1730 by the Independents. It was situated in front of the site of the 11th century St. Owen's Church, that was pulled down at the time of the Civil War siege of Gloucester in 1643, when suburbs were fired as a military tactic. Services ceased in 1974 and the chapel demolished in 1981.

74 In 1867 Samuel Moreland began making lucifers in his small factory premises adjoining the Gloucester-Berkeley Canal in Bristol Road, later to be England's Glory. Women and children were employed as outworkers, making match boxes. The Moreland family continued to run the business after it was acquired by Bryant & May in 1913, until 1972. The factory closed in 1976. Raw materials and finished products were delivered and despatched cheaply and quickly by canal and river. This photograph, taken about 1895, shows one of Moreland's fleet of horse-drawn wagons used for delivering matches to Birmingham and the Black Country. Motor vehicles took over in 1919. The ship at the centre of every box-label is H.M.S. *Devastation*, launched in 1871, a twin-screw, iron turret battleship of revolutionary design.

75 As Gloucester's industrial output increased, so did the need for more housing. From the mid-1890s the City corporation encouraged speculative builders to lay out streets for residential development on its land in the Stroud Road/Tuffley Avenue areas. These semi-detached houses in Tuffley Avenue represent the styles prevalent at that time. With the increase in population in this area, the need for improved transport led to the City's tramways being extended to Tuffley Avenue in 1897.

76   This memorial, that now stands in Sydenham Gardens, Stroud Road, originally stood in the middle of the highway at the junction of Southgate Street, Bristol Road and Stroud Road. It was moved to its present position in 1923. It is in the form of an Elizabethan three-sided fountain and in its original position carried no fewer than nine water-spouts. There were a drinking fountain and a horse-trough. It was erected in memory of Thomas Nelson Foster, a citizen who helped to make the city prosperous at the turn of the century. He owned the oil and cake mill in Merchants Road.

77   Standing just inside Southgate Street, the photographer looks down Northgate Street in about 1900. On the northwest corner of the Cross can be seen Hargreaves, the chemist, later to become the site for the London City & Midland Bank. On the northeast corner can be seen Manns, the jewellers, established in 1741, who continued to trade at the same premises until fairly recently. The man talking to the policeman on duty seems to be attracting the bystanders' attention.

78   The London City & Midland Bank has now taken up residence on the northwest corner of the Cross in this postcard dated about 1915. The electric trams have been running since 1904. The posts carrying the overhead wires have been made decorative features of street furniture. A delivery van unloads at Southerns, a well-remembered grocery store to the right of the bank.

Northgate Street from the Cross, Gloucester.

79 When the Royal Agricultural Show was held in Gloucester in June 1909, it became a historic occasion when Edward VII chose to visit it, being the first formal visit of a reigning monarch since 1788. The show was held on the Oxlease below Westgate Bridge. Arriving at the G.W.R. Station, the King went to the Guildhall for a civic reception before proceeding through a highly decorated City centre to the showground. The Cross in particular, seen here, was very elaborate; flags, bunting and floral works of art greeting him wherever he chose to glance.

80 Taken before the days of the electric trams, one of George Symond's horse-drawn omnibuses stands in Northgate Street. Three paper boys idly pose for the photographer outside Southern's grocery stores. At first-floor level a large tea-caddy can be seen, the traditional sign of a tea-merchant.

81   Though the New Inn Hotel has 'Motor Entrance' on its sign-board, there is no motor in sight, but there are still plenty of horse-drawn conveyances in this view of Northgate Street dated 1909. There are some well-dressed ladies doing their shopping, none of whom would care to be seen without a hat. All the buildings seen along the right side of the street have been considerably altered, or replaced.

82   Cars are regularly being seen on the City streets and the New Inn Hotel boasts an Automobile Association sign in this view, taken about 1912. The prominent gabled building on the left was Boots, the chemist, which moved to Eastgate Street in the 1980s. It had a very decorative mock-Tudor frontage, and was built just before the First World War. All the buildings to its left have been altered or rebuilt, the principal building occupying the area being Marks & Spencers, built in the 1930s. Nothing moved at any great speed so it was safe to wander in the roadway.

83   Into this courtyard of The New Inn, Northgate Street, came the carriages, or in earlier times, the stage coaches to drop off or pick up passengers and change horses. It probably was, and still is, one of the largest buildings in the City. The New Innn has been described as the finest example of a medieval galleried inn in Britain, still much admired and photographed by tourists today. It was built as a Pilgrim's Hostel by the Abbey of St. Peter in the 1450s to accommodate visitors flocking to see the tomb of Edward II within the Abbey Church. He had been cruelly murdered in Berkeley Castle in 1327.

84   In this view of the courtyard, looking east, creeper hangs down in curtains and drapes the upper galleries. The entrance leads into a second courtyard to stable the horses and park the coach more securely. The yard was a popular place for travelling players of bygone days, the steps and galleries making an ideal stage. Plays are still sometimes performed there today. From the steps public proclamations were occasionally made instead of at Gloucester Cross. In the time of James I, we are told, the New Inn even boasted its own tennis court.

85   A picture of the original Bon Marche – now Debenhams – taken around the late 1920s. With the exception of the two buildings on the left, the whole area was demolished to enable the present building to be constructed. The business was founded in 1889 by Mr. John Rowe Pope and remained in the hands of the Pope family until 1971. The narrow lane on the right was Oxbode Lane. This was widened when the new store was built.

86   Northgate Street at the junction with St. Aldate Street on a sunny summer's day with the shop awnings down to protect the goods in the window, providing potential customers a shady spot to view the wares on offer. The picture was taken at the end of the last century, when horse-drawn omnibuses were the public form of transport. A part of the classical 18th century frontage of St. John the Baptist Church peeps out on the right.

87   The horse-conveyance in St. Aldate Street is heading towards Northgate Street, passing the church of St. Aldate on its left. In the 13th century there was the church of St. Aldhelm, which became called St. Laurence in the 14th century. It was demolished in the 1650s. The parish remained without a church until a simple brick building in Gothic style with a belcot was opened in 1756. By the 1930s the church had been converted into a Parish Hall until its removal in 1963. The building, then Coles & Sons, decorators, to be seen at right angles to the street beyond the church, is all that remains on the left of the street today.

88   Sunday in Northgate Street. All the blinds are down in the shop windows and not a horse, cart or tradesman in sight. The spire of St. John's Church takes centre stage – all that remains of the earlier medieval church. The body of the church was rebuilt in 1730-1734 to a basilican plan with a well-proportioned classical east front, designed by Edward and Thomas Woodward of Chipping Campden. Recent redevelopment to the right side of the street has been sympathetic to the fabric of this old street.

89 An old-fashioned chemist shop on the corner of Northgate Street and Worcester Street kept by Mr. J. Curtis, who is seen standing in the doorway. At the time this photograph was taken, about 1906, there were six chemist shops in Northgate Street. The premises are now occupied by a firm of estate agents. The sign of the barber is visible – a hairdressing establishment still exists almost in the same position.

90   A hot summer's day, 1905 – notice the horse's head-gear. Northgate Street at the junction with Worcester Street. One can feel the pace of life at that time – no faster that the plod of the horse, the pushing of the barrow. Conway-Jones, decorators, elegantly advertise on a gable end. The tower of St. Peter's Church sits loftily in the centre of the photograph.

91   A group of youngsters pose outside the Wesleyan Chapel, Northgate Street, in 1889. Built in 1877 by Charles Bell, this imposing structure replaced an earlier chapel built in the 1780s, where Wesley preached on several occasions. Congregations of 450 to 650 people by the 1850s led to the need for a larger building for worship. Rather in the style of Wren, the twin towers, imposing portico and large rose window presented a magnificent sight when entering town from Worcester Street. Dwindling congregations caused the closure and subsequent move to St. John the Baptist Church in 1972 which, under a sharing agreement with the Anglicans, was called St. John's Northgate. A supermarket was built on the site.

92   The Black Dog inn seen in this postcard dated 1905 is the point at which Northgate Street used to end and London Road begin – before the construction of Black Dog Way in 1966 when the building was demolished. A great black dog 8 ft long and 4 ft high lay on the parapet, shortly after this photograph was taken, for about sixty years, enhancing the name of the inn. Carved out of teak by the celebrated Gloucester sculptor Arthur Levison, it replaced an earlier dog fashioned from petrified oak. The dog had been lost for years, assumed destroyed, but was found in Stroud and might one day return to Gloucester.

ST. PETERS, R.C. CHURCH.

93 A postcard of the ivy-clad Roman Catholic Church of St. Peter in London Road, built in 1860-1868 by Gilbert Blount in an early 14th century style, replacing a small brick chapel built in 1792 behind a house on this site, dedicated in 1851 to St. Peter ad Vincula. The presbytery beside it was built in 1880. The steeple is a delight when approaching up London Road, the open bell stage with coupled arches on each side giving a splendid airy effect. The stained glass and painted sanctuary are by Clayton & Bell, but were later toned down by Linthont of Bruges in 1939, except in the Lady Chapel.

94   An attractive picture of the shop at 35 London Road occupied by the Goddard family. Originally the family had what was described as a 'Pianoforte Manufactory' in Northgate Street, in premises which were also used as an Assembly Room, which, in about 1909, were to become the Theatre de Luxe. Today the theatre site is a restaurant in a cul-de-sac.

95   A picture of yesteryear. A horse-drawn omnibus plying up London Road approaching Heathville Road on the left. This picture was taken in 1882, some three years after the trams had started to operate. The glasshouse was part of Paradise Nursery owned by Roberts & Starr, who had a shop at 92 Northgate Street. On the right and within about a hundred yards of each other were three public houses: the York House inn, the New Inn and the Denmark Arms.

96   A typical street scene of the 1920s. Taken in London Road near the entrance to Oxford Street, the tram is on its way to Elmbridge Road from The Cross. The old railway bridge is clearly seen. The horse-drawn vehicle on the left was more than likely a local baker's delivery van.

M323   GLOUCESTER CAR No.7

Pamlin Prints
Croydon CR0 1HW

97 Northgate Manse, the rectory for St. John's Church, Northgate Street, lay near the corner of Heathville Road/London Road and had been acquired for the Rector in the early 1870s. There were many houses used by the clergy in London Road. In 1906-1907 Reverend Crake was in residence.

98   Whereas London Road today mainly consists of offices and a few residential properties, at the time of this postcard it was particularly favoured by the middle-class, the shop owners and city clergymen. In 1814 some substantial detached villas were being built and again in the 1840s. Suburbs grew up alongside London Road in Anglo-Saxon times, but were destroyed during the Civil War in 1643. By 1780 there were a few scattered houses, along with the ancient hospitals of St. Margaret and St. Mary Magdalen, which were rebuilt as almshouses in the early 1860s.

99   Probably the most elaborate Victorian building in Gloucester, Hillfield House in London Road, is set in a large garden with well-kept trees and flowerbeds, now a public park. In the 1820s a large villa was erected here, with extensive grounds. It was rebuilt to an Italian design much favoured by the Victorians in about 1867 by Albert Estcourt. More and more it came to be used for offices – in this postcard as the Diocesan Church House. In 1915 it was used as a Red Cross Hospital for war-wounded soldiers. In 1933 the City corporation acquired the house and grounds and it is now used as government offices.

100   This long expanse of road is that going uphill to St. Catherine's Church, Wotton, from Barnwood Road. Only one of the further houses on the right remains and the gardens of Bohanam House to the left are now public gardens. The tram ran from Gloucester Cross to Hucclecote.

101 Party rivalry during the 1850s parliamentary elections was apparently fuelled by concern over increasing corporation expenditure. The Conservatives sold some corporation property to raise funds and pay off debts to the Charity trustees, carried out Board of Health and Burial Ground works, and built a new Produce Market, Corn Exchange and Cattle Market. They also constructed a part of Denmark Road, seen here in 1909. There had been a few houses built for more prosperous residents at the entrance to the road (then known as Gallow's Lane) in the 1840s. In the 1890s large houses continued to be built with in-filling by speculative builders and the laying out of new streets.

102 An aerial view of Denmark Road (centre) and surrounds, taken about 1930 before the estates were developed. The houses on the left are those in Hinton and Malvern Roads, some of which were erected just before the turn of the century. The open area to the right of the houses was Sir Thomas Rich School's playing field. The Kingsholm Recreation Ground and the Gloucester Rugby Ground are clearly identified. Middle left is the Girl's High School, and bottom right houses are just being constructed in Estcourt Road.

103   This fine 16th century timber-framed building, seen in this postcard in 1886, was the Raven Tavern in Hare Lane. It was an important inn, situated on the 'Great North Road of the West of England', which passed the Royal Palace at Kingsholm. At the beginning of the 19th century a wider road was built to take this traffic, called Worcester Street, and Hare Lane became a quiet side-street. In the late 1930s many clearances and rehousing schemes took place in the old areas of the City, such as Hare Lane. Sir Philip Scott saved the old tavern from destruction and it was restored by H.F. Trew. It is now an old peoples' club.

104   St. Lucy's Home of Charity was founded in 1864 by Thomas Gambier Parry. Its aim was to train nurses and to tend the sick and needy in their own homes. The Sisters of St. Lucy were an Anglican community, taken over in 1872 by the Sisters of St. John from Clewer (Bucks). In 1876 Gambier Parry moved the home to this large house pictured on the left, at the corner of Hare Lane and Pitt Street. They ran a children's hospital, an orphanage, and a reformatory in this and other homes. In 1885 a ward for fee-paying incurables was added. In 1879 a club was founded by Constantia Ellicott, the bishop's wife, to train factory girls for domestic service. St. Lucy's Home closed in 1933 following the withdrawal of the Clewer Sisters. After demolition the area became a small public open space, designed by John Holman, known as St. Lucy' Gardens.

105   The Probate Court or Registry was built in 1858 to a Gothic design by Thomas Fulljames & F.S. Waller. It stands on the corner of Pitt Street and Park Lane, where it continued to deal with all matters of *the Probate, Divorce and Admiralty Division of the High Court of Justice* – to give it the full 19th century title – until the court was moved to new premises on Kimbrose Corner, in Southgate Street, in 1994. In the late 1920s King's School occupied the first floor of the left-hand section.

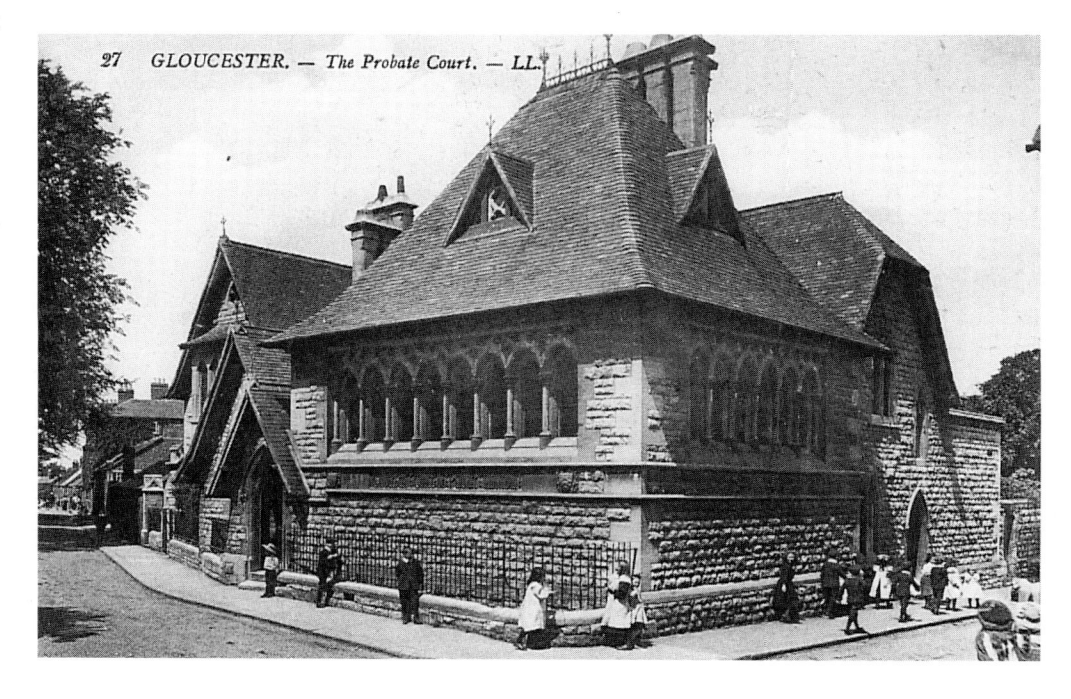

106   The first Sunday School in England was held in this old house in St. Catherine Street in 1781. It was situated in the northern suburbs of old Gloucester. Some free elementary education started with the Poor's School founded in 1700, but these early Sunday Schools were to have a significant effect, and what Robert Raikes started here in Gloucester, in partnership with Reverend Thomas Stock, curate of St. John's Parish, gave an impetus to the National Sunday Schools Movement. They employed women to teach in the poor areas of the city, where the poverty had promoted the idea. Children aged between 5 and 14 were taught reading, spelling and had religious instruction.

First Sunday School for Boys, Gloucester

107   The Girl's Sunday School was founded a few years after the Boy's school in this delightful old house on the corner of Park Street and St. Catherine Street. For many years the building carried a plaque stating that it was the first Girl's Sunday School. This was one of several charitable projects carried out here in Gloucester – establishing a County Infirmary in 1755 and building a 'model' prison in 1791 being two others. Because of the prevalent philanthropic spirit, Gloucester escaped the serious problems of poverty and unrest seen in the Midlands and London. The house was demolished in the 1950s.

108 The tram plies up Worcester Street in this view dated 1915. In the 1820s a barrister, John Phillpotts, promoted the building of a new, wider road to be called Worcester Street, to replace the narrow, congested Hare Lane. It was financed by tolls on all road users and was carried out under the powers of the Tewkesbury Road Turnpike Trustees.

109   The Ecclesiastical Parish of St. Marks, Kingsholm, was formed in 1846 from the parishes of St. John the Baptist, St. Mary de Lode and St. Catherines. The church, seen here in about 1909, was erected in 1846 by the Diocesan Church Building Association, designed by Francis Niblett in an Early English style.

110   This postcard of the interior of St. Marks, Kingsholm, shows the Lady Chapel and the new organ that were added to the building following its restoration in 1898, the chancel having been altered in 1890. The east window, by Kempe, was added in 1895, and the west window was by Willement. This church is frequently used today for the funeral services of true gypsies, which tend to be very colourful affairs.

111 A much favoured public house, not only by the local residents but also by the rugby fans, who each week flocked to the ground on the opposite side of the road to watch the 'Red & Whites' in action. Judging by the list of organisations who had their headquarters at the inn, it must have been a very popular rendezvous. The inn, still in business, although very much altered, was owned by Godsells of Stroud, who were acquired by The Stroud Brewery Co. and later by Whitbread.

112   An enthusiastic team and official members of the City Albion A.F.C. taken during the 1924-1925 season. They had their headquarters at the Kingsholm inn and the landlord, A.V. Byard, was the treasurer.

113   A healthy group of children pose for the camera in Kingsholm Road in 1917. Much of this road developed in the 1850s and 1880s with substantial villas and terraced houses. The toll house, just visible behind the children, was erected in 1822 by the Tewkesbury Road Turnpike Trustees in order to charge tolls to improve the northern route into the City. During the reign of Edward the Confessor the Great Hall of the Royal Manor or Palace at Kingsholm became the regular meeting place of the King and his great Council. When William the Conqueror built Gloucester Castle to the southwest of the town, the palace ceased to be used. Fame returned to this area in 1891 with the 'Red & Whites', the Gloucester Football Club.

114   A picture of the Free Hospital for Children of the Poor at Kingsholm. It was founded in 1867 by Thomas Gambier Parry of Highnam Court and in the main was supported by voluntary contributions. An out-patients dispensary was also provided. After closing as a hospital in 1947 it was sold to the corporation and became a nurses' home. It was demolished in 1979 and a housing estate built, called Gambier Parry Gardens.

115   Two youngsters and a delivery boy pose in this postcard, dated 1906, of All Saints' Church in Lower Barton Street. Designed by Sir George Gilbert Scott in 1874, Pevsner in the 'Buildings of England' series declares it to be the finest 19th century church in Gloucester and a good example of Scott's work. It was built for the west part of St. James' Parish, the cost being met by subscription and a benefaction from the family of Thomas Hedley, the first perpetual curate of St. James. The stained glass is by Clayton & Bell.

116   The Choir of the Good Shepherd Church, Derby Road, taken in May 1931. The church was a Chapel of Ease for All Saints' adjoining the former railway crossing in Barton Street. It was in a very populous area and well-supported. Clergy from All Saints' undertook the ministry of the church. In the centre of the picture is Reverend C.W. Janvrin. The church was built in 1892 of brick and timber, designed by Waller & Son, the cathedral architects. It was sold in 1974 to a community of Ukrainian Catholics.

117 This early picture of Barton Street shows the houses and shops built from the mid-19th century. On the left is the Vauxhall Inn, which had been part of the pleasure grounds known as Blenheim Gardens. Opened in 1812, it was much frequented in the 1820s where there were a bowling green, tea gardens and events such as balls and pigeon-shooting matches. In its first years there were firework displays to celebrate the Peninsular War victories. It was renamed Vauxhall Gardens in about 1832, but only the bowling survived behind the Vauxhall Inn until the mid-20th century. The gardens were covered with terraced houses from 1863, but were immortalised in the streets Blenheim Road and Vauxhall Road.

118   Gloucester park, a large area of open space south of the City, was frequently used for the celebration of major local or national events, such as this occasion, to commemorate the Coronation of King George V in June 1911. No expense appears to have been spared to ensure this day of national holiday would be remembered for a long time to come, judging by this elaborate carousel. Out came the Sunday best and the hats, an entertainment in themselves. But what a serious looking lot – not a smile to be seen amongst them.

119 This postcard shows the cinema in Park End Road, which later became the Elim Pentecostal Church. The Park End Hotel can be seen opposite on the right, which is on the corner of New Street. It was a residential street and had the tram from Gloucester Cross to St. Barnabas Church, Tuffley, plying its length.

120   This very popular cinema in Park End Road was opened in 1914. It belonged to James Maysey and was later operated by Cinema House Ltd. and Gloucester Cinemas Ltd. In 1926, before the introduction of the 'talkies', it had an orchestra under the direction of a then well-known musician, William Bird. After the cinema closed on 27th April 1957, it became the Elim Pentecostal Church.

121   St. Paul's Church in Park End Road was built as a memorial to Robert Raikes soon after the centenary in 1880 of the Sunday School Movement. It was designed by Capel N. Trigg, the son of a Gloucester timber merchant and a pupil of James Medland, who established his own practice in the early 1870s, but died in 1883 at the early age of 38 years. It was built to relieve pressure on the churches of St. James and St. Luke. Of rusticated limestone in the Early English style, it was unfinished at its consecration. The incomplete south tower is now used as a porch. The stained glass in the east window is by Hugh Easton.

122   The labourers pause for a few moments to have themselves photographed, along with a few 'willing helpers', whilst undertaking the laying of the tracks for the Electric Tramway System at the junction of Park Road, February 1904. The trams came into service on 4th May. St. Paul's Church can be seen in the background.

GLOUCESTER ELECTRIC TRAMWAY CONSTRUCTION, FEBRUARY, 1904.
Stroud Road with Park End Road Branch.

DANCEY, Publisher, Gloucester.

123   A rise in population during the 19th century as a result of increased industrial activity in the City and surrounds led to the creation of many new streets and housing, such as we see here in Conduit Street, in the 1880s and 1890s. A talk with the three folk standing at their front door could reveal much about an era long past.

124   Off the south end of Lower Barton Street, Moor Street was in the midst of a densely built-up area. This scene of flood water photographed in 1924 allows us to catch a glimpse of the residents that we might not otherwise have seen. It has given the youngsters some fun, even if the adults may have wished it further. The Sudbrook flows through this area and a sudden, heavy summer storm has probably caused it to overflow its banks.

125   The New Inn at Tuffley – a family favourite. A ride on the tram to Reservoir Road and then a short walk along Stroud Road brought one to this old-fashioned inn. It is now completely reconstructed and re-christened 'The Fox and Elms'; perhaps such an evocative name can bring back memories of more rural days.

126 The outlying parish of Hempsted lies by the River Severn southwest of Gloucester. St. Swithun's Church was founded in early Norman times and in the Middle Ages Hempsted was one of the estates of Llanthony Priory. At the junction with Rea Lane is this late medieval village cross, possibly that for which William Franklin left money in 1417 before setting out on pilgrimage to Compostella.

127   This gateway situated in Hempsted Lane is all that remains of Llanthony Priory. The mother-house was in the Honddu Valley, mid-Wales, and was being frequently raided, so in 1136 they set up a so-called temporary house here in Gloucester. By the 14th century they were in financial difficulties following a fire in the church. Despite being rebuilt, this church was said to be ruinous by 1518. The site was sold by the Crown in 1540 and was used as a residence until 1697, and then as a farmstead. During the late 1790s the Gloucester/Berkeley Canal was dug through the east side of the Priory precincts.

128 The Port of Gloucester is the most inland port in Britain, and although it has undergone a radical change of use, its Victorian atmosphere persists to this day. This postcard shows the close proximity of the Docks to the City centre. The Gloucester/Berkeley Canal, 16 miles in length, was especially suited to the sailing ships and coastal steamers that traded between this country and continental ports, up to 1,200 tons burden. There was ample warehousing for grain and general goods, cranes and winches for dealing with all classes of cargo, connections to the main line railways and two graving docks. Birmingham and the Midlands were easily reached by the river north of Gloucester.

GLOUCESTER, GENERAL VIEW FROM AN AEROPLANE (853)

129 From the mid-19th century to today the Midlands was the scene of the most varied and extensive industrial enterprises in the U.K. The Inland Waterways system proved to be the quickest and cheapest highway for getting raw materials and manufactured goods to and from their destinations before improvements were made to the road and rail networks. Vessels up to 250 tons burden could lock down into the river from the Docks at Gloucester and proceed to Worcester, the Midlands and Black Country. Here goods are being transhipped from the barge *Nelson* to a narrow boat of the Severn & Canal Carrying Company, formed in 1873, to continue the journey northwards.

130   Gloucester was one of the largest timber-importing centres in the U.K., drawing its supplies from the Baltic, Canada, Norway and Russia. Woodworking, an important city industry, included furniture and cabinet making, doors and windows, ladders and matches. Here deals are being unloaded from a steamer at Roman's Yard about 1925. J. Romans & Co. had a large timber yard adjoining Llanthony Road. Most of the other timber yards were down the east bank of the canal, occupying continuous frontage of ³/₄ mile. Today most wood arrives by road. Price, Walker & Co. Ltd., one of the largest importers of soft woods, dates back to 1736.

131   A busy scene in 1909 taken from the bridge at Llanthony looking south down the canal. The warehouse was known as the Pillar Warehouse, constructed in 1838 with the front of the upper storey supported on pillars, providing a covered wharf. Jointly financed by Samuel Baker – hence Baker's Quay – and James Shipton, it was used by corn merchants J. & C. Sturge. In the distance can be seen Foster's Gloucester oil mills, that processed linseed, cotton and groundnut oils for animal feed. To the right can be seen wagons standing in the G.W.R. goods yard and tarpaulin works.

132   This postcard was probably produced following the opening of the Midland Station, later called Eastgate, in 1896. For 'steam-buffs' the locomotive is an M R *Kirtley* 2-4-0. Kirtley was the first locomotive engineer of Midland Railway from its formation in 1844-1873. His design of a fire-box capable of burning coal instead of coke had considerable influence on the development of steam engines. A similar Kirtley engine can be seen at the Midland Railway Centre, Butterly, Derbyshire, saved from the breakers on withdrawal in 1947.

133   The Royal train stands at the platform of the Great Western Railway Station, later the Central, when King Edward VII visited the Royal Agricultural Show at Gloucester on 23rd June 1909. Until Midland Station opened its new station further to the southeast in 1896, the M.R. terminus lay close to the G.W.R. Station. A long covered footbridge was built connecting the two stations that remained in use until 1975. Only the Central Station remains. Such was the individuality between the two companies, extreme inconvenience was caused at Gloucester due to different gauges, necessitating a change of train for passengers and goods travelling between Bristol and Birmingham. In 1854 M.R. converted the Bristol line to narrow-gauge and built the Tuffley, or Barton, loop-line into its Gloucester terminus.

134   The Wellington Hotel is still situated right beside the railway station, which at the time this photograph was taken, was the Great Western Railway Station, or a four minute walk along the covered walkway would bring one to the Midland Station. Only a few minutes from the City centre, it was well placed for both businessman or visitor. In the early city guide books it was described as 'a first class Family Hotel replete with every comfort and convenience; electric light in every room. Under the personal supervision of the sole Proprietor, Henry Braine.'

135   After the dreadfully fetid, damp, disease-ridden prisons of an earlier era, this purpose-built prison, designed by William Blackburn, in Gloucester, was a model for national reform. Opened in July 1791, the key word apart from security was 'ventilation'. Fresh air came through iron grills set in floors, ceilings and walls. Here the Black Maria brings a batch of prisoners to the Lazaretto, another innovation. At this entrance lodge, new arrivals received a bath, health check and had their clothes fumigated as a further measure to prevent the spread of disease.

136 A relic of past years – Eton jackets, mortar-boards, bowler hat. A group photographed outside the Cloisters entrance of Gloucester Cathedral during the Three Choirs Festival, September 1925. The three choristers (left to right) are Reg Woolford (co-author of this publication), Cyril Gwynn, the youngest of four brothers all of whom were Cathedral choristers, and Cecil Hibbins. P.C. Wigmore, the gentleman with the bowler hat, Mr. W. Evans (Cathedral Head Gardener), and the other gent (left), a car park attendant, were engaged for the Festival Week as ticket collectors.

137   A photograph of some King's School pupils taken outside what was then the main school buildings in the Cathedral Gardens. In the late 19th, early 20th century it was a small academically undistinguished school of fifty to sixty boys run by the Dean and Chapter, principally as a Choir School. Today it is classed as an Independent Cathedral School. This picture was taken on Speech Day 1924. Those with shining faces were obviously prize winners. The boys wearing Eton collars were choristers.

138 A group of King's School pupils taken in 1928 in the Cathedral Chapter House. The school was expanding very rapidly and additional accommodation was used, including a part of the Library. Amongst the pupils were Kenneth Williams, who was one time Vicar of Stroud; Geoffery Fowler, who was a partner in the law firm of Scott & Fowler; Tom Southern, who had a shop in Northgate Street, an old established firm of grocers. In the back row sits the co-author of this publication.

139   The Derby Road Schools were opened on 8th April 1907 by the Mayor, Samuel Aitken, and provided accommodation for 1,100 children: boys, girls, and infants, built by the City council which had become the local education authority in 1903. In 1925 the Boy's and Girl's Schools housed the Central Schools, set up by the council to provide technical and industrial training for children aged 11 and over. The school closed in 1957.

140 Many charitable organisations were doing good works in the Victorian era and helping crippled children had long been a feature of life here in Gloucester. Organised by the Adult Schools' Union, six coach-loads packed full of excited children head for the Sharpness Tea Gardens in June 1910.

OUTING OF POOR CRIPPLED CHILDREN OF GLOUCESTER
(TO SHARPNESS TEA GARDENS, JUNE 18th, 1910).
Organised by Adult Schools' Union. President, H. Money; Secretary, F. W. Viner; Treasurer, J. Embling.
(Photo by Leonard E. Hopkin, 9 Midland